HOW TO BE FUNNY

An A to Z of amazing and
astonishing ways to make people laugh

Would you rather see your friends rolling in the aisles,
splitting their sides, or laughing the house down? This
comic collection of do-it-yourself humour will tell you
everything you'll ever need to know to achieve riotous
results! Here, together for the first time in one volume,
are all sorts of jokes, funny stories, zany plays, crazy
cartoons, loony games – and much, much more. Read it
from A to Z and become a Fun Expert – if you can stop
grinning, giggling and guffawing long enough yourself!

D0569284

How to be Funny

illustrated by Colin Hawkins

An A to Z of amazing and astonishing ways to make people laugh

Gyles Brandreth

Hippo Books
Scholastic Publications Ltd
London

Scholastic Publications Ltd,
141-143 Drury Lane, London WC2B 5TG England

Scholastic Book Services,
50 West 44th Street, New York 10036 NY USA

Scholastic Tab Publications Ltd,
123 Newkirk Road, Richmond Hill, Ontario L4C 3G5
Canada

H J Ashton Co Pty Ltd, Box 579,
Gosford, New South Wales, Australia

H J Ashton Co Pty Ltd,
9-11 Fairfax Avenue, Penrose, Auckland, New Zealand

Made and printed in the USA

CONTENTS

ANYONE CAN DO IT!

Making people laugh is a wonderful gift. Some people have it naturally – and are funny without having to think about it. But most of us aren't that lucky. We'd like to be funny because it is such fun being funny, but we aren't quite sure of the best way to set about it. That's why I've written this book. It is packed with practical ideas, games to play, jokes to tell, silly poems to recite, all of which should help you to make your family and friends smile, chuckle and even occasionally roar out loud!

You can be funny in so many different ways. Telling funny stories is probably the most popular, and jokes come in all sorts of shapes and sizes. You can learn the Quick Quip:

A bee's just a humbug!

or the Short Story:

There were two men riding on a train for the first time ever. They had some bananas they'd brought with them to eat on board. Just when they were peeling the bananas the train went into a very dark tunnel.

The first man shouted out in the darkness, 'Have you eaten your banana yet?'

'No,' the friend replied.

'Well, don't touch it!' warned the first man. 'I took one bite and went blind!'

Then there is the Long Joke, which is too long to put here, so I won't mention it! (See 'Long Jokes'.) You need to memorise Long Jokes carefully and make sure you deliver the punchlines clearly and with just the right emphasis. Never rush through the story and never tell the same Long Joke to the same audience twice.

Practise your jokes as much as you can — it's only by trying out different ones that you'll learn which kind you tell best. You might find that people laugh at you more when you tell Long Jokes rather than Quick Quips, or when you do funny things; you'll just have to experiment.

Sometimes people laugh at you when you're *not* trying to be funny. Although it may be annoying for you to drop a heavy book on your toe, everyone watching could find it hilarious — even your friends. After the first yelp of pain try to laugh with them, and keep them laughing with a joke — the one about the man who dropped a detective story on his toe, shouted in pain and said angrily, 'I thought it was supposed to be *light* reading!'

With a bit of luck people will also laugh at you when you try to do funny things. These can be very simple, like wearing a false nose or mask, or something that takes worthwhile time — putting on a play, organising a treasure hunt, or dressing up.

I was brought up on the saying 'There's a time and place for everything,' but there are very few occasions when humour does not help. If a friend is ill, you can try cheering him up with your collection of printing errors (see 'Hold the Front Page!' and 'It Pays to Advertise!'). If your younger brother or sister is bored, amuse them with 'Ridiculous Riddles'. If your mother is annoyed at you for spilling orange squash all over her best sofa, you could try to make her smile with a joke:

'Doctor, doctor, I feel like a dog.'
'Well, sit down and tell me about it.'
'I can't, doctor, I'm not allowed on the furniture.'

However, this might make matters worse – so be careful!

Serious things can be faced more easily if you can find the humour in them. Going to the dentist can be a very serious business, but try to remember the funny side:

'I said DON'T
SWALLOW'
yelled the dentist.
'That was my *last*
pair of pliers.'

That couldn't have really happened (could it?), but some very odd things *do* happen in real life, and sometimes even make the papers! There was the report, for instance, of a man who went to bed, stubbed his cigarette out on his plastic false teeth, and started a blaze so huge that the fire brigade had to come and put it out. All you have to do to be funny is to keep a watchful eye on the news, and remember things like that.

People also *say* very strange things. I was visiting a school recently and heard someone explain, 'I always find my feet are too big for other people's stairs ...' If you hear it, write it down! Keep a notebook handy and everywhere you go be ready to jot down things that strike you as funny: odd road signs; the funny things you hear on buses; silly advertisements on hoardings or on the television; funny things that happen to you. The more you look, the more you'll see – watch the way people talk, walk, behave. Listen to what they say and how they say it. Mike Yarwood studies his subjects closely before making us all laugh with his brilliantly accurate impersonations.

Whatever you do, DO NOT make jokes at someone else's expense. Don't try to be funny if your best friend's dog has just been run over. WAIT UNTIL THE TIME IS RIGHT before you launch into your jokes, impersonations and charades. And DO watch people carefully to see what makes them laugh. When others are chuckling at the television or in the cinema you should keep one eye on them and remember the sort of thing that amuses them most. After all, their idea of what's funny may be different from yours. To be really funny, you have to be able to make *everyone* laugh, so the more you watch, listen, write down and memorise the better at it you'll be.

Have fun!

BEST BAD JOKES

'Bad' means that these jokes will make you groan rather than laugh – it doesn't mean that they're no good! Lots of people love Bad Jokes because they know just what to expect.

What is all this groaning really about? A lot of it is caused by odd words called 'puns'. To explain a pun, it's best to demonstrate how one works. You ask, 'Why do leopards never escape from the zoo?' The answer is, of course, 'Because they're always spotted.' 'Spotted' means both that they have spots and that they are seen. This is a pun, and for you to make your own Bad Jokes, you need to know how to make puns, too. Some useful words to start with are:

saw	change
ruler	dough (doe)
horse (hoarse)	light
well	spring
roll	great (grate)

As you see, the words don't have to be spelt the same as long as they sound the same. Sometimes you can have words that are quite different:

Did you hear about the cat who swallowed a ball of wool? SHE HAD MITTENS!

So, as well as learning these jokes by heart, make up your own; and when your chance comes you can start telling them in a long breathless string, not waiting for anyone to laugh before you go on to the next! That way, you'll never know whether they would have laughed, groaned or stayed silent!

What do you do if someone offers you rock cakes?
Take your pick.

What animal is it best to be on a cold day?
A little otter.

What language do twins speak in Holland?
Double Dutch.

What does the sea say to the sand?
Nothing, it just waves.

If you dug a hole in the middle of the road what would come up?
A policeman.

Why are oysters lazy?
Because they are always found in beds.

How many peas are there in a pint?
One.

What would happen if you swallowed a frog?
You might croak.

What kind of puzzle makes people angry?
A crossword puzzle.

Did you hear about the fight on the bus?
The conductor punched a ticket.

Why is an operation funny?
Because it leaves the patient in stitches.

What do you say to a man who is 2 metres tall and in a nasty temper? SIR.

What kind of bulbs should you never water?
> *Light bulbs.*

Why does the Statue of Liberty stand in New York Harbour?
> *Because she can't sit down.*

How was spaghetti invented?
> *Someone used his noodle.*

What would you do if you swallowed a pen?
> *Use a pencil.*

What's the first thing you put into a pie?
> *Your teeth.*

What happened at the flea circus?
> *A dog came and stole the show.*

Is it true that a lion won't attack you if you're carrying an umbrella?
> *That depends on how fast you're carrying it.*

What is a three-season bed?
> *One without a spring.*

What tree does everyone carry around with him?
> *A palm.*

What did the dirt say when it rained?
If this keeps up, my name's mud.

How is a doormat related to a doorstep?
It's a stepfather.

How can a leopard change its spots?
By moving.

Why did the boy sleep on the chandelier?
Because he was a light sleeper.

Why did the store hire a cross-eyed man as detective?
Because the customers wouldn't know which way he was looking.

FOREMAN: 'Why are you only carrying one plank when the other men are carrying two?'
WORKER: 'Well, they're too lazy to make a double journey like I do.'

JUDGE: 'You claim you robbed the grocery store because you were starving. So why didn't you take the food instead of the cash out of the till?'
ACCUSED: 'I'm a proud man, Your Honour, and I make it a rule to pay for everything I eat.'

TEACHER: 'Are you good at arithmetic?'
PUPIL: 'Yes and no.'
TEACHER: 'What on earth do you mean?'
PUPIL: 'Yes, I'm no good at arithmetic.'

'My youngest boy is troubled with rheumatism.'
'That's bad — how did he get it?'
'He didn't get it — he can't spell it.'

'Did any of your family ever make a brilliant marriage?'

'Only my wife.'

GUEST: 'Does the water always come through the roof like that?'

HOTEL MANAGER: 'No, sir, only when it rains.'

PATIENT: 'Doctor, will I be able to play the violin when my hand is healed?'

DOCTOR: 'Yes, certainly.'

PATIENT: 'That's good – I never could before.'

A farmer's pig was knocked over by a motorist and killed. 'Don't worry,' said the motorist. 'I'll replace your pig.'

'You can't,' roared the farmer, 'you're not fat enough!'

LITTLE BETTY: 'How long is it to my birthday, Mummy?'

MOTHER: 'Oh not long now, dear.'

BETTY: 'Well, is it time for me to begin being good?'

'Did you have any difficulty with your Italian in Rome?'
'No, but the Italians did.'

MUSEUM CURATOR: 'Please be careful of that vase.
It's 2,000 years old.'
MOVING-MAN: 'Sure I will, sir, I'll be as careful as
if it were new.'

'What have you done to your face?'
'I had a little argument with a bloke about
the traffic!'
'Why didn't you call a policeman?'
'He WAS a policeman.'

The office manager pointed to a cigarette butt on his
office floor.
'Is this yours, Carruthers?' he said sternly.
'Oh, not at all, sir,' said Carruthers, 'you saw it first.'

INDIGNANT MOTORIST: 'I had the right of way
when this man ran straight into me, officer, and yet you
say I was responsible. How do you account for that?'
POLICE OFFICER: 'His father is the mayor, his
brother is the chief constable, and I'm engaged to his
sister.'

FATHER: 'You're always wishing for something you
haven't got.'
SON: 'Well, what else can one wish for?'

GERTIE: 'This match won't light.'
BERTIE: 'It did a minute ago when I tried it.'

**Man on telephone to fire chief: 'You can't
possibly mistake it – it's the only burning house
on the street.'**

'Did anybody drop a roll of money with a rubber band round it?' asked the man in the bank.
'Yes, I did,' piped up several voices.
'Well, I just found the rubber band,' said the man.

A young lady came to the doctor in distress. 'I've broken my glasses. Do I have to be examined all over again?'
'No,' said the doctor, 'just your eyes.'

'Are your fish fresh?' asked the customer.
'Of course they're fresh madam,' said the fishmonger. Then, turning round to the slab, 'Keep still, can't you!'

'What's your name?' the policeman asked the Irish driver.
'It's on the side of me van, Officer.'
'It's obliterated.'
'Oh no, sorry, Officer, it's O'Reilly.'

Old Lady (seeing tug-of-war for the first time): 'Wouldn't it be simpler if they got a knife and cut it?'

CUSTOMER: 'Waiter, I can't eat this soup.'
WAITER: 'I'll get the manager, sir.'
CUSTOMER: 'Manager, I can't eat this soup.'
MANAGER: 'Sorry, sir. I'll get the chef.'
CUSTOMER: 'Chef, I can't eat this soup.'
CHEF: 'What's wrong with it?'
CUSTOMER: 'Nothing – I haven't got a spoon.'

Lady to new daily help: 'Mrs Briggs, did you sweep behind that door?'
Mrs Briggs: 'Oh yes, ma'am – I sweep everything behind the door.'

MOTHER: 'Have you given the goldfish fresh water?'
WILLY: 'No – they haven't drunk all their old water yet.'

SUE: 'What kind of husband would you advise me to take?'

BERYL: 'Take a single man and leave the husbands alone.'

LITTLE WINNIE: 'How much a pound do people pay for babies?'
MOTHER: 'Babies aren't bought by the pound, dear.'
WINNIE: 'Then why do they always weigh them as soon as they're born?'

FOR SALE
BEST OFFER
OVER 50p

EMMA: 'Mummy, Jimmy broke my doll.'
MOTHER: 'Oh the naughty boy – how did he do that?'
EMMA: 'I hit him on the head with it.'

MR SHOW-OFF: 'Have you ever hunted bear?'
MR BLOGGS: 'No, but I've hunted in my shorts.'

MRS PROUD: 'My son has been playing the violin for five years.'
FRIEND: 'Dear me, his arms must be very tired.'

Customer at hardware store: 'Who's in charge of the nuts here?'
Assistant: 'Just a moment sir, and I'll take care of you.'

TEACHER: Did your father help you with this arithmetic?
BRIAN: No, Miss, I got it wrong all by myself.

DAN: 'My mother thinks I'm too thin.'
TOM: 'What makes you say that?'
DAN: 'She says she can see right through me.'

DOLLY: 'My mother can play the piano by ear.'
BILLY: 'That's nothing – my dad can fiddle with his moustache.'

Little Suzie had been in the sun and was peeling badly. She ran to her grannie, saying 'Look, grannie, only four years old and I'm wearing out already.'

CONFUCIUS HE SAY

'Confucius, he say ...'

You've probably heard people tell jokes that begin like this. Confucius was in fact a real person – a Chinese thinker who lived fifteen hundred years ago. His wisdom was considered to be very great, though his sayings seemed – at first glance – very straightforward. They seemed so simple when translated into English that some people made fun of them by taking up the line 'Confucius, he say ...' and making jokes. These jokes started off as folksy sayings, and there's usually half of the old saying left. Have a look at the ones below. You should be able to make some up, too – just take a popular saying, such as 'Look after the pennies, and the pounds will look after themselves' and give it the Confucius treatment!

A friend in need is a big nuisance.

He who laughs last doesn't get the joke.

You can fool some of the people all of the time, and all of the people some of the time – but for the rest of the time they will make fools of themselves.

To err is human – so is covering it up.

No legs are so short that they won't reach the ground.

It is better to have loved a short girl than never to have loved a tall.

No artist is so bad that he can't draw his breath.

Do unto others before they do unto you.

Better to keep your mouth shut and have people wonder if you're stupid than to open it and remove all doubt.

Life's like a shower – one wrong turn and you're in hot water.

Early to bed and early to rise means you never see anyone else.

An apple a day keeps the doctor away – if it's thrown in the right direction.

The early bird catches the worm – but who eats worms, anyway?

rasp

You can take a horse to water, but if you can get him to skin-dive, then you've *really* got something.

DAFT DEFINITIONS

Dictionaries are not usually very funny things, but then, they're not meant to be. However, they are useful if you want to find words for Daft Definitions.

All you do is take an everyday word and give it a funny new meaning. So, if you have 'carpet' you might find the Daft Definition, 'a hamster in a car'! Or perhaps 'slate' which means 'it isn't early' (it's late!)

Here are some more. You'll soon get the idea and be able to make up your own:

LAZYBONES
A skeleton that doesn't like work.

OUT OF BOUNDS   A kangaroo suffering from exhaustion.

HALFWIT   Somebody who's funny half the time.

FREE SPEECH   Using someone else's phone.

DOCTOR   A person with inside information.

JET-SETTER   A fast-flying dog.

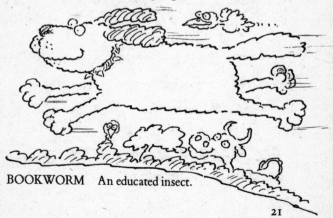

BOOKWORM   An educated insect.

SEASICKNESS   What a doctor does all day.

UNDERCOVER AGENT   A spy in bed.

WATERMELON   A fruit that you can eat, drink and wash your ears with at the same time.

WHOLESOME   The only thing from which you can take the whole and still have some left.

CABARET   A row of taxis.

RHEUMATIC   An apartment at the top of a house.

WORSHIP   A battlecruiser belonging to the Mayor.

DISCOVER   Case for a gramophone record.

DATA   Make an appointment with a lady.

CONVERSION TABLE   A piece of furniture that folds up into something else.

MISINFORM   A schoolgirl.

DECORATION   A speech on board ship.

LUNATIC   A tiny insect who lives on the moon.

BEEHIVE   Stop acting that way.

DOGMA   A dog's mother.

SATELLITE   To commit arson.

ACCURATE   A vicar's assistant

GROAN   Became larger.

ENTERTAINMENT

Here we have some entertaining ideas for entertaining your family and friends. You might like to set up a small stage – or at least have a space surrounded by chairs where you can try these out.

MUSIC

For a very easy and amusing concert you can play musical glasses. Fill eight glasses with water. Tip out some of the water from each glass and then tap each with the handle of a wooden spoon. You should get each one to play a different note. When you've done this, try playing a simple tune such as 'Three Blind Mice'. To add to the fun of the performance, have a whistle in your mouth, and a saucepan lid to bash every now and then. The results may not be great music, but they should be great fun!

MAGIC

To be funny at magic is quite tricky! The best way is to learn some simple tricks from a book of magic and then, when you 'perform' them, pretend to be very clumsy and do everything wrong. There are lots of things that will look funny on stage: tripping over and dropping your pack of cards; having a goldfish bowl full of water for a trick and then dropping coins, or buttons into it by mistake; wearing big braces that get caught up in your magic wand. One accident should follow another until, just when everyone is in stitches, you do the trick properly so the performance comes to a neat end.

VENTRILOQUISM

Again – do it wrong! To be a good ventriloquist takes many years of training, but to be a bad funny one takes only a few minutes.

Unless you're very lucky, you won't be able to use a proper dummy, but you can make one from an old sock and two round sticky labels. Put the sock on your right hand and push a bit of it between your thumb and forefinger to make a mouth. Peel the two labels off their backing and stick them on above the mouth. You now have your dummy! You can move your thumb about to give the impression that the dummy is speaking, but the funniest bit will be what you say to each other. You must try to do the dummy's lines without moving your lips and without laughing, but exaggerate the difficulties of making the dummy sound normal, and bring in lots of misunderstandings. For example:

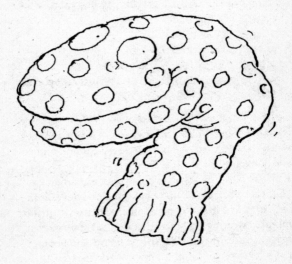

DUMMY: It's windy today isn't it?

YOU: No, it's Thursday, I think.

DUMMY: No, no. Windy. WINDY.

YOU: I'm sure it's Thursday.

DUMMY: Oh! So am I – what have you got to drink?

YOU: What would you like?

DUMMY: Some geer.

YOU: Some what?

DUMMY: Some geer. A gottle of geer.

YOU: You mean, some *beer*. Why didn't you say 'beer' instead of 'geer'?

DUMMY: I can't say 'guh'.

YOU: You mean 'buh'.

DUMMY: That's right, 'guh'.

YOU: Well, you'll have to do the best you can. Would you like a big bottle of beer or a small one?

DUMMY: I'd like a gig gottle of geer.

YOU: What?

DUMMY: A small one.

And so on!

FORTUNE-TELLING FUN

Fortune-telling can be fun. Of course, no one actually
believes in all that stuff. Only this morning I met a
gypsy who told me I was going to have an accident
and ...

AAAAAAaaargh!!!!

(NORMAL SERVICE WILL BE RESUMED AS
SOON AS POSSIBLE. DO NOT ADJUST YOUR
BOOK! We will be with you again just as soon as we
have pulled the author out from under the
chandelier ...)

Where was I? Oh, yes. I was about to say that fortune-telling is a very serious business. It's not something to be trifled with or made fun of. So, why don't you take a rest from all this being funny business for a while and be Deadly Serious and learn to become a Fortune-Teller? To help you, we have produced a script. This is to give you an idea of what to do.

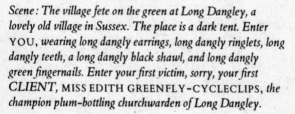

★ ★ THE CRYSTAL BALL ★ ★
Act One Scene One

Scene: The village fete on the green at Long Dangley, a lovely old village in Sussex. The place is a dark tent. Enter YOU, *wearing long dangly earrings, long dangly ringlets, long dangly teeth, a long dangly black shawl, and long dangly green fingernails. Enter your first victim, sorry, your first* CLIENT, MISS EDITH GREENFLY-CYCLECLIPS, *the champion plum-bottling churchwarden of Long Dangley.*

YOU: Come in, my dear, and sit down. I see you are troubled ... or was it too much ginger beer in the Refreshment Tent?

MISS E: Are you really Gypsy Rose O'Beans?

YOU: I am indeed she. Sit down, my dear, and take the weight off your plates. That's plates of meat, I mean. Feet. Never mind, dear, just sit down.

MISS E: Can you see into the future?

YOU: If you cross my palm with paper, I can. Especially if it's a five pound note — I can see very well then.

   [MISS E *gives you a fiver*]

YOU: I shall gaze into my crystal ball. What do you wish to know?

MISS E: Can you see what's going to happen next year at the Long Dangley Plum-Bottling Championships?

27

YOU: I see mists. And more mists. And more mists. And a dark man ... it's Bert Ford. It must be the weather forecast. Ah, now the mists are clearing. I can see something else. It's a man. A man coming towards you.

MISS E: [*shrieks*] A man?

YOU: Yes, I see a long dangly man. I mean, a man from Long Dangley. He's tall, dark and ugly ... it's the vicar!

MISS E: [*shrieks again*] The vicar!!

YOU: Yes. He's judging the plum-bottling. He's come to your plums now. He's tasting them.

MISS E: [*further shrieks*] Have I won?

YOU: He's passing on ... he's talking to a man dressed in a tablecloth ... he's an Arab. He's won! Yes, he's won! He's a Sheik!

MISS E: [*shrieks*] A Sheik!

YOU: He's won it. He's won it with his jar of pickled sheep's ears!

[MISS E *flounces out in a huff, which was knitted for her by her aged aunt,* LADY KNITS-BADDLEY *of Lacey Pullovers, Dorset.*]

★ ★ Tea and Tarot
Act One Scene Two ★ ★

Scene: A dismal tea-room. The waitress, tables, chairs and cake-trolley are covered in cobwebs. The clock stopped in 1938 and the service a long time before that. Into this gloomy scene steps ... fresh-faced Health Food fanatic and Vegetarian MISS TRISHIA NUTTER. *In the corner of the tea-shoppe, amongst the cobwebs ... something stirs. ... yes! It's* YOU!

YOU: I can see by your eyes that you have trouble ahead.

MISS N: A glass of apple juice and two prune cookies, please.

YOU: I told you so.

MISS N: Are you the waitress?

YOU: No, I'll call her. Waitress! Two teas and a Tarot pack, please. No, my dear, I'm the Reader in Tea Leaves. One glance into your cup and I can see what's in store for you.

MISS N: Really? How super! O.K. then!
[*She drinks her tea*].

YOU: [*chanting magically*]:
Abracadabra, and Sneezlegum,
Toasted tea-cakes and brownies –
The tea-leaves that have touched your lips
Will now reveal your future.

MISS N: But that doesn't rhyme!

YOU: Rhyming's extra. Aha! I see something terrible in store for you.

MISS N: Wh–What is it?

YOU: A leg of lamb.

MISS N: A leg of lamb?

YOU: Yes, yes. A leg of lamb, and it will do you great harm.

MISS N: Never! I will not let it pass my lips! I shall never eat a leg of lamb again!

YOU: That won't matter, it's going to fall on your head and . . .

AAAAAAAAAARGH!!!!
[*Unfortunately, and unpredictably, your chair collapses, and you have to end the Fortune-Telling for the day*].

CURTAIN

In olden times, people tried to forecast the future in some very odd ways. The Ancient Greeks had something called the Oracle. This was a voice that lived in a cave. It spoke only if presents were brought, so it was quite a clever voice. No one ever saw the owner of the voice. It was a very well-kept secret.

There aren't many Oracles about today — not ones that live in caves, anyway. You could have one, although it would have to live in a cellar or a cupboard and not a cave, and it wouldn't be just a voice — it would be you! Invite your friends to question the Oracle about very important things, such as:

'What's for tea today?'
           or:
'Who's going to win the Cup?'

You, the Oracle, should be hidden so that you can be heard but not seen. When you are asked a question you should have some special way of answering. For example, the answers to the second question above might be:

When moons go green from too much pop!
    When chips fry on the grill!
Then EVERTON will win the Cup,
    But Arsenal never will!

Your friends will either storm your 'cave' or shout out, 'WHAT??!' If so, you should call out quickly, '3–1'.

There are, of course, the trusty old tea-leaves. When you pour your tea, don't strain it! Drink as much as you possibly can, then chuck away the rest of the tea. There should be tea-leaves left at the bottom of the cup.

If you look at them for a while you should be able to see something – a ship (which might mean you're going on a long journey), or a bicycle (which might mean you're going on a short one). You might see anything, but if there's nothing there at all, it means either that the future is very blank, or your mother's using tea-bags to make the tea!

I see a tall dark stranger

GypsyMoth
Bag reading
50p

GAMES THAT RAISE A LAUGH

Another way to entertain your friends is to show them how to play Funny Games. You must be sure about how the games are played, though. You won't be very popular if you begin a game which you can't finish. Go through these games first just to make sure you will be able to explain to others how to play them.

THE PICTURE FRAME GAME

This rib-tickling game is nice and simple. Just find an old picture frame and with your friends watching you, hold it in front of your face so that you're framed! You musn't laugh or even smile, because you're supposed to be like one of those serious portraits you see in art galleries. The more serious you look, the more your friends will laugh; but then, if you laugh too, ask one of them to try it and see if he can do better!

THE LAUGHING GAME

This is another simple game, in which you have to choose a victim. Once you've got one, tell him he has to look stern even though you're all going to try to make him laugh. This can be done in any way — by making funny noises, or strange faces. If he does laugh, someone else must take his place.

FAMILIAR FACES

This calls for a little bit of preparation. Look in newspapers or magazines for familiar faces wearing funny expressions. Cut them out and stick them on a big sheet. Give each a number. Your friends then try to guess the names. They might recognise Princess Anne in an ordinary photograph but will they know her when she's eating sour fruit? You can have pictures of famous football players, or cricketers, or television people, or politicians – of anybody at all, as long as they all have funny looks on their faces.

BITE THE PENNY

This is a messy game so put a large sheet, or several pieces of newspaper on the floor. Fill a large, shallow bowl half-full with flour. Then bury about half a dozen washed, dry pennies in the flour. (Make sure they are really dry or the flour will get gluey.) The unfortunate penny-biter must now get the pennies out of the flour using his teeth, but nothing else. (When it comes to your turn, the knack is to blow away the flour until the penny can be picked up easily. Don't dive in!)

Get some of your friends to lie on the floor, and cover them with a sheet, leaving only their bare feet sticking out. Give the rest paper and pencils, and going from left to right, get them to write down who the feet belong to.

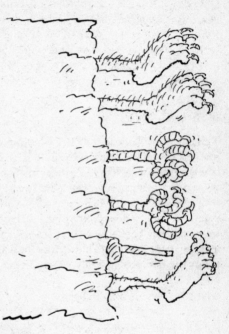

CROSSBREEDS

This is a good game for two people. Draw the top half of a person or animal, and then fold the paper over so that only a very small amount shows. Next your friend draws a bottom half on to your drawing – and you do the same for hers. Then you unfold both drawings and have a good laugh at the strange sort of animals you've created!

This game can be quite hilarious – you have freedom to choose your beneficiaries* and your bequests** but you don't know what you are bequeathing – until later.

You will need a sheet of paper for each person playing, marked out as follows:

I,   being of
unsound mind do hereby will and bequeath:

1.   my
     to
     so that (s)he will

2.   my
     to
     in the hope that (s)he will

3.   my
     to
     and ask that (s)he will

4.   my
     to
     on condition that (s)he will

*Beneficiaries are the people to whom you leave your possessions in your will.

**Your bequests are what you leave them.

35

The space after 'my' you leave blank but after the word 'to' you write the name of the beneficiary (this can be a friend, a television personality, or even Battersea Dogs Home).

On the last line write the reason for the bequest, i.e., 'So she can keep warm in the long winter evenings', or 'In the hope that it will keep him in at nights'.

When the forms have been completed each person is given a list of bequests and inserts one after the word 'my' in each case.

Then you read out your own will!

Some sample bequests:

Empty yoghurt carton	Roller skate
Old toothbrush	Athlete's foot
Garden gnome	Dustbin lid
Join-the-dots book	Mickey Mouse badge
Dead goldfish	Apple core
Tin mug	Wine gums
Old plimsoll	Broken zip
Gumboil	Frog spawn
Macaroni	Cracked gramophone
Old school tie	record
Cockroach collection	Mary Poppins cricket pads
Slice of Mother's Pride	Old tram ticket
Completed crossword	Irish penny
puzzle	Stale fish-finger
Lolly-stick	Banana skin
Catfood	Beechams Pills
Soggy cornflakes	Odd sock
Gorgonzola cheese	Blazer button
Library ticket	Coca-Cola tin
String vest	Safety pin
Picture of Queen Victoria	Busted lamp bulb
Damp tea-bag	Stained beer-mat
Castor oil	Dracula outfit

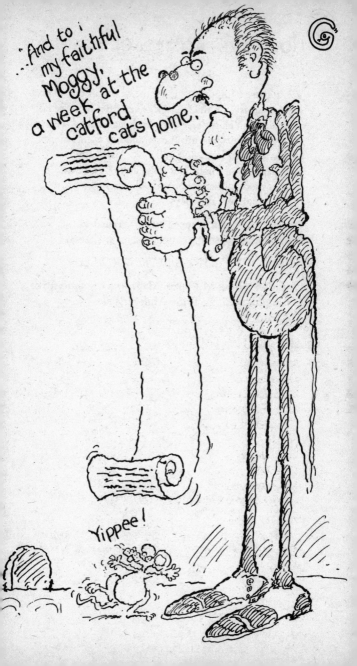

HOLD THE FRONT PAGE!

When there's important news, the newspapers will keep some space free on the front page and fill it in at the last moment with all the latest details. Because they are in a hurry, misprints and misunderstandings occur. Here are some real examples. If you look closely at your newspapers you might spot some gems like these. Collect them in a scrapbook so you can make your friends laugh on rainy days.

On board the train, trapped by falls of earth at Wilmington, were $1\frac{1}{2}$ passengers, mostly female.

NEW COUNCIL SETTLES DOWN WELL

One of the newer M.P.s rushed across the floor to shake a clenched fish in the Prime Minister's face.

PENGUIN TO PROTEST AT ANTARCTIC TALKS

Ice-cream vendors, expecting big earnings in the next few days, have arranged for huge socks to supply the city.

SHEILA IS THE FIRST LADY TO TAKE OVER THE TOAST AND MARMALADE SHOW, WHICH HAS ALWAYS BEEN A MALE PRESERVE.

WHEN WASHING WINDOWS, ADD A SMALL
AMOUNT OF VINEGAR TO THE WATER. THIS
WILL KEEP THE FLIES AWAY AS WELL AS
CLEANING THEM.

AN AMERICAN MUSICIAN WAS FOUND IN A
DOORWAY HOLDING A HAMMER,
SCREWDRIVER AND SPANNER AT 3.0 A.M. HE
TOLD POLICE 'I WAS JUST GOING TO MAKE A
GUITAR'.

In spite of the snags that bedevil every big exhibition the
British Museum's spectacular display of gold and silver
dating from AD 300 to 700 opens tomorrow.
Preparations for handling crows of Tutankhamun
dimensions were well in hand yesterday.

THIS IS A QUIET NEIGHBOURHOOD WITH DOGS AND CHILDREN RIDING BICYCLES.

Not all of the cars recalled had defects. For instance, General Motors recalled 32,640 Buicks, Oldsmobiles and Pontiacs to find 1,250 which had been fitted with wheels.

WILL LADIES KINDLY EMPTY TEAPOTS, RINSE ROUND, AND, BEFORE LEAVING, PLEASE STAND UPSIDE DOWN IN THE SINK.

Notice is given fixing the charge for the use of the WC at the zoo in the Bois de Vincennes at 3 francs. This new tariff will take effect retrospectively as from 1 July last.

The seats in the vicinity of the bandstand are for the use of ladies. Gentlemen should make use of them only after the former are seated.

40

IT PAYS TO ADVERTISE!

Advertisements go wrong, too! These odd ads can be put in another part of your scrapbook or you can copy them and put them in a folder. It's a good idea to put down the name of the paper you found them in. This adds interest and can be very funny – there's a paper in Australia called the *Toowoomba Chronicle*!

THE DUN COW REQUIRES FULL TIME SNAKE WAITRESS.

1929 ROLLS ROYCE HEARSE FOR SALE. ORIGINAL BODY.

LOST-BLIMPTON AREA. BLACK LONGHAIRED BUTCHER'S ASSISTANT. IF FOUND WANDERING RING 4925 - REWARD. SENTIMENTAL VALUE ONLY.

DUE TO FALL OUT ACROBAT REQUIRED.

ENTERTAINMENTS – CLOWN JOEY (PLEASE SEE 'DEATHS' COLUMN).

WANTED: GRAND PIANO FOR WOMAN WITH CARVED MAHOGANY LEGS.

BED AND BREAKFAST, REASONABLE RATES,
COMFORTABLE BEDS, HOT AND COLD
RUNNING WAITER IN EVERY ROOM.

DECORATOR – SPECIALISES IN INFERIOR
WORK. IMMEDIATE ATTENTION.

CRASH COURSES ARE AVAILABLE FOR THOSE
WISHING TO DRIVE QUICKLY.

INTELLIGENT YOUNG LADY WANTED FOR
INTERESTING AND RESPONSIBLE WORK.
MUST BE PROPER GOOD AT GRAMMER AND
SPELLING.

HELP WANTED : MAN WANTED TO HANDLE
DYNAMITE. MUST BE ABLE TO TRAVEL
UNEXPECTEDLY.

WOODFORD SOCIETY ANNUAL CHEESE
AND WIND PARTY WILL BE HELD NEXT
SUNDAY EVENING.

FOR SALE OAK TABLE WITH STRONG LEGS
AND VANISHED TOP.

FOR SALE TERRACED HOUSE BRICK BUILT
WITH STALE ROOF.

CHARLADY REQUIRED FOR LIGHT
HOUSEWORK AND HOVERING.

TUTOR OFFERS O AND A LEVEL POACHING
TO EXAM CANDIDATES.

LOVELY HOLIDAY COTTAGE. SLEEPS SIX.
ONLY FIFTEEN MILES WALK TO THE SEA.

Beefburger & chips	....	80p
Egg and chips	....	60p
Sausage and beans	....	70p
Children	....	50p

WANTED – SINGLE-HANDED CHEF FOR
LUXURY HOTEL IN LAKE DISTRICT.

RENT A POLAR BEAR CHEAP. EATS
ANYTHING. VERY FOND OF CHILDREN.

The best funny men have a joke for every occasion – a story that fits every topic. To help you, we proudly present our Joke Encyclopaedia, an A–Z of different subjects, each with its own joke.

A

AIRPLANE

Aboard an airplane high over the Atlantic Ocean:

'Ladies and Gentlemen. This is your Captain speaking. I've some good news and some bad news. First, the good news. We have perfect visibility, clear weather, we're making record time and we'd be there in half an hour if it weren't for the bad news which is, we're lost.'

B

BAND

CUSTOMER: 'Will the band play anything I ask them to?'
WAITER: 'Yes, sir.'
CUSTOMER: 'Well, ask them to play cards.'

C

CAKE

MOTHER: 'Why are you cleaning up the spilt coffee with cake?'
GEORGE: 'Well, Mum, it's sponge cake!'

CANNIBALS

The trouble with cannibal jokes is that they aren't in good taste.

D

DOCTOR

A husband took his wife to the doctor.
HUSBAND: 'Doctor, my wife thinks she's a chicken.'
DOCTOR: 'That's terrible. How long has she been like this?'
HUSBAND: 'Three years.'
DOCTOR: 'Why didn't you bring her to see me sooner?'
HUSBAND: 'We needed the eggs.'

DUCK

JO: 'We went over a duckway last night.'
JILL: 'What's a duckway?'
JO: 'About five pounds.'

E

ELEPHANT

PATIENT: 'Can a person be in love with an elephant?'
DOCTOR: 'No, it's out of the question.'
PATIENT: 'Do you know anyone who wants to buy a very big engagement ring?'

EYES

DOCTOR: 'Have your eyes been checked in the last few months?'
PATIENT: 'No, Doctor. They've always been plain blue.'

F

FISH

What fish has a good ear for music?
   A piano-tuna!

FOOT

JAMES: 'I'll never be able to leave you.'
RACHEL: 'Do you like me that much?'
JAMES: 'No. You're standing on my foot.'

G

GRAVES

When an old Red Indian called Short Cake died, his tribe argued about who should dig his grave. In the end, his widow settled it. She said, 'Squaw bury Short Cake.'

H

HAIR

FATHER: 'Oh, dear. I think my hair's getting thinner.'
MOTHER: 'Don't worry – nobody likes fat hair.'

HORSE

The God of Thunder went for a ride on his favourite filly. He cried out, 'I'm Thor!'
The horse said, 'Well, you forgot the thaddle, thilly!'

I

INVISIBLE MAN

NURSE: 'Doctor, doctor. The Invisible Man's here.'
DOCTOR: 'Tell him I can't see him.'

J

JAIL

The sword swallower's in jail again – he hiccupped and stabbed two people.

JUDGE

JUDGE: 'The next person who raises his voice in this court will be thrown out!
PRISONER: 'Hip, hip hooray!'

KING KONG

ARTHUR: 'I can trace my ancestors all the way back to royalty.'

BILL: 'King Kong?'

L

LADDER

JUDGE: 'What do you mean by bringing a ladder in here?'

PRISONER: 'I want to take my case to a higher court.'

LOONY

BUS CONDUCTOR: 'Come down, there's no standing on top of this bus.'

LOONY: 'Why not?'

BUS CONDUCTOR: 'It's a single-decker.'

M

MILLIONAIRE

From the will of a miserly millionaire: '... and to my dear nephew whom I promised to remember in my will, "Hello, there, Bill!"'

MUSIC

COMPOSER: 'Why do you play this bit of music over and over?'

PIANIST: 'It haunts me.'

COMPOSER: 'I'm not surprised. You've murdered it often enough.'

N

NAILS

'At last I've been able to make my son stop biting his nails.'

'How did you do it?'

'I made him wear shoes.'

O

ONIONS

JIM: 'Did you hear about the man who lived on onions alone?'

JACK: 'No, but anyone who does *ought* to live alone!'

OPERATIONS

SURGEON: 'How is the patient feeling after his operation?'
NURSE: 'Fine, except that we can hear a double heartbeat.'
SURGEON: 'Oh, so that's where my wristwatch went!'

P

PIANO TUNER

PUZZLED MAN: 'I didn't call for a piano tuner.'
PIANO TUNER: 'No, it was your neighbours who sent for me.'

POISON

Did you hear what happened to the scientist who mixed poison ivy and a four-leaf clover?

He had a rash of good luck.

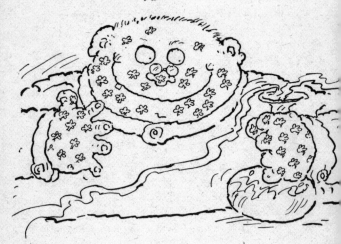

Q

QUESTIONS

What has never asked a question, but still gets plenty of answers?

    A doorbell!

R

RESTAURANT

FIRST TRAMP: 'I know a restaurant where we can eat dirt cheap.'

SECOND TRAMP: 'I don't like dirt!'

S

SLEEP

PATIENT: 'Doctor, doctor, I can't sleep at night.'

DOCTOR: 'Lie on the edge of the bed and you'll soon drop off.'

T

TEACHER

TEACHER: 'John, what comes after the letter "A"?'

JOHN: 'All the rest of 'em.'

TRAIN

PASSENGER: 'I don't know why you bother to have timetables – your trains are always late.'

GUARD: 'Well, how would you know if they were late if you didn't have a timetable?'

UMBRELLA

JIM : 'When should a mouse carry an umbrella?'
JACK : 'When it's raining cats and dogs.'

UNDERWEAR

TONY : 'Are there any holes in your underwear?'
MIKE : 'What an insult! Of course there aren't.'
TONY : 'Well, how do you get your feet through?!'

V

VEGETARIANS

Once upon a time there was a tribe of vegetarian cannibals. They were very fussy. They would only eat Swedes.

W

WAITER

CUSTOMER : 'Waiter, do you have frogs' legs?'
WAITER : 'Of course, sir.'
CUSTOMER : 'Then leap over the counter and get me a drink.'

WEREWOLF

GEORGE: 'Mummy, Mummy, all the kids say I look like a werewolf!'

MUMMY: 'Shut up, George, and comb your face.'

X

XMAS

FRED: 'What did the fireman's wife find in her stocking at Christmas?'

BERT: 'A ladder!'

X-RAY

PATIENT: 'What does the X-ray of my head show?'

DOCTOR: 'Nothing.'

YELLOW

DAN: 'What's yellow on the inside but green on the outside?'

GRAN: 'A banana disguised as a cucumber.'

ZOO

What do you get if you cross an elephant with a goldfish?

Swimming trunks!

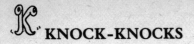

KNOCK-KNOCKS

People have been having fun with Knock-Knock jokes
for over half a century. Over the next fifty years you
can make your family and friends laugh by trying out
your Knock-Knock jokes on them. Here are some
examples to inspire you.

Knock, knock.
Who's there?
Lion.
Lion who?
Lion here on your doorstep. Open up.

Knock, knock.
Who's there?
Lydia.
Lydia who?
Lydia teapot.

Knock, knock.
Who's there?
Eileen.
Eileen who?
Eileen'd on the fence and it broke.

Knock, knock.
Who's there?
Norma Lee.
Norma Lee who?
Norma Lee I wouldn't trouble you but I need help.

Knock, knock.
Who's there?
Esther.
Esther who?
Esther anything I can do for you?

knock knock

Knock, knock.
Who's there?
Thea.
Thea who?
Thea later, alligator.

Knock, knock.
Who's there?
Sonia.
Sonia who?
Sonia bird in a gilded cage.

Who's a pretty Sonia then?

Knock Knock

Knock, knock.
Who's there?
Jester.
Jester who?
Jester song at twilight.

Knock, knock.
Who's there?
Sacha.
Sacha who?
Sacha lot o' questions …

Knock, knock.
Who's there?
Theresa.
Theresa who?
Theresa Green.

Knock, knock.
Who's there?
Eddie.
Eddie who?
Eddieboddy in there?

Knock, knock.
Who's there?
Sharon.
Sharon who?
Sharon share alike.

Knock, knock.
Who's there?
Watson.
Watson who?
Watson your mind?

Knock, knock.
Who's there?
Arthur.
Arthur who?
Arthur any more at home like you?

Knock, knock.
Who's there?
Señor.
Señor who?
Señor mother out and let me in.

Knock, knock.
Who's there?
Bernardette.
Bernardette who?
Bernardette all my dinner and I'm starving.

Knock, knock.
Who's there?
Lionel.
Lionel who?
Lionel get you nowhere – better spill the beans.

Knock, knock.
Who's there?
Juno.
Juno who?
Juno what time it is?

LONG JOKES

Long Jokes are called Shaggy Dog stories. This may be
because Shaggy Dogs have long coats, or perhaps ...
well, it doesn't matter. The thing is that long stories are
not only more difficult to remember, but they're much
more difficult to tell than short ones. Your audience will
quickly get bored unless there's something funny at the
beginning. So, it's best to choose stories that have funny
or odd subjects, like the one about the gorilla in a coffee
shop. This way the audience will wonder what the
punch line is going to be, so you'll keep their attention
until the end. That is, as long as you memorise the joke
well – and don't fluff it! If your Shaggy Dog story is
met by a great groan or, worse, a stony silence, it is best
to follow it straightaway with some jokes from the
'Quick Quips' section!

THE GORILLA JOKE

A gorilla went into a coffee shop, sat down and ordered
a coffee. The waiter was a bit nervous at first, but there
weren't any other customers and the gorilla seemed
quite friendly, so he let him sit in peace. Who'd argue
with a gorilla, anyway?

While the waiter made the coffee, he watched the gorilla from the kitchen. The gorilla just sat there, staring at the ceiling. The kettle boiled and the waiter made a fresh cup of coffee and took it in. The gorilla handed him a five-pound note, and proceeded to drink the coffee. The waiter took the five-pound note and went back to the kitchen to get some change. While he was there he watched the gorilla, who drank the coffee, but for the rest of the time just stared at the ceiling. The waiter thought to himself, 'That gorilla won't know the difference between a pound note and a five-pound note – he's only a gorilla, after all ...' So he took a pound note and went in to give it to the gorilla. As he handed it over, he said:

'We don't get many gorillas in here.'

The gorilla took the pound note and replied:

'I'm not surprised, with coffee at four pounds a cup.'

THE QUIET WEEKEND JOKE

A farmer came back home after a weekend in the city, and was met at the station by his farmhand.
    'How's everything, Fred?' asked the farmer.
    'Oh, so-so.'
    'Anything much happen?'
    'Nothing to speak of. The dog limps a little.'
    'How's that, then? How'd that happen?'
    'The horse kicked it running out of the stable. He must have been a bit crazy, being half-singed.'
    'Half-singed?'

'Yes. Well, when the barn burnt down, all the hay and stock got burned, except the horse – and I had to shoot him later, he was so singed.'

'How did the barn catch fire?'

'A few sparks from the house, I think. That was what woke me – one of your daughters screaming upstairs that the house was on fire.'

'Oh – house went too? Did you save anything?'

'Oh yes. When I woke, the whole kitchen was ablaze, but I unlocked the front door. Then I remembered your case of whisky in the shed behind the kitchen, and I knew you wouldn't want anything to happen to that. When I got it out it was too late to save the two girls, or the three boys, or the baby, or even your wife. I suppose your parents were crisped to a cinder straight away – but I saved the whisky.'

'Well, that's something. Anything else happen?'

'No. It was a pretty quiet weekend, really.'

It can be great fun to make-up and dress up – and it's another excellent way of being funny. Remember to ask before using any of the bits and pieces lying round the house. If you don't, and they turn out to be priceless, you could be in real trouble. You'd need more than this book to make your parents laugh if you cut up your grandmother's silk scarf to make Lawrence of Arabia's head-gear!

If you look through all the old cupboards, wardrobes and attics in your house, you're bound to find lots of things you can use to dress up in. Here's a list of people you can dress up as:

LAWRENCE OF ARABIA – an old dressing-gown, a tea towel for your head-dress, kept in place by a dressing-gown cord or a tie.

DRACULA – a dark blanket for a cloak, black suit or jersey and trousers underneath. Make yourself some fangs out of cardboard.

A GHOST – you should be able to find an old white sheet or table-cloth, and if it's really old, ask if you can paint a ghastly, staring face onto it.

MAKE-UP

Dressing up and parading around is terrific fun. But
why not do the thing properly and try make-up, too?
Ask your mum or sister if you can use some of theirs.
There are lots of weird and wonderful things you can do
with make-up. Here are a couple of sample make-up
plans:

A COMEDY SHOW

Now you've got the hang of costume and make-up,
why don't you go the whole hog and put on a comedy
show for your friends and family? Get together and
plan it with a few other people. Try and keep it full of
short bits, not a long-drawn-out play — just in case
things go wrong! It's easier to give up a little sketch and
race on to the next, rather than try and rescue a long
and involved play that's gone wrong. Short sketches are
much funnier, too!

One of the acts could be a stand-up comic who simply came on and told jokes. But it would be a lot funnier if you did it in some kind of costume – say, a clown (pyjamas and clown make-up) or even Superman!

As another act, you could perform little sketches with two or three other people. Use some of the jokes in this book. You could act out any of the 'Doctor, Doctor' jokes on pages 45–46, with a doctor and a patient doing several of the jokes in a row. Or act out some charades – you'll find some suggestions for animal ones in the 'Zoo Time' section on page 106. If you think ahead and plan them carefully, you can make them really funny!

Just a word of warning. Don't be so keen on the idea of dressing-up that you plan a show full of too many weird and wonderful costumes. Remember that changing into costumes takes absolutely ages, and you don't want to keep your audience waiting – even if it's only Mum and Dad dozing on the sofa! Have a fantastic costume of course, but wear it throughout or plan carefully how to have time to change out of it if you need to. Waiting for performers who are taking ages changing can be *very* boring!

If the audience have enjoyed themselves, they may want to give you a bit of extra pocket-money as a token of appreciation – if so, why not give it to a charity? In fact, you could make Christmas happier for lots of people by doing a series of these comedy shows in your friends' houses, collecting for Oxfam or Save the Children. Why not? After all, being funny can spread happiness in all sorts of ways!

NUTS IN MAY

You can be Nutty in May – or June – or July, or in any month for that matter! Especially April, when it's April Fool's Day!

Make people laugh by doing nutty things; balancing an eel on the end of your nose isn't easy – but mastering a Funny Walk is.

Here are some suggestions for ways to be nutty all the year round.

FUNNY WALKING

You've probably seen Charlie Chaplin walking his funny walk – a sort of side to side movement made funnier because his shoes are so big and awkward to manage. Your funny walk can be 'aided' by a pair of your father's shoes – if you can walk safely in them. Carry a walking-stick, or pretend to carry a tray of tea-cups. Let your legs go wild when you walk – swing each leg as far backwards and forwards as it will go without you losing your balance. Try to make each step the same – that is, make each leg do the same things every time you take a step.

BARMY NOISES

Get a friend to play the Barmy Noises game with you. One of you has to think of some very unlikely thing, and the other has to illustrate it without any outside help.

The sort of thing for which you have to make the right noises could be the sound of a sockful of custard being blown through a wind tunnel and hitting a cow.

WELLY-THROWING

Lots of nuts throw wellies. They throw them at tea-pots, or trees, or over hurdles made of bits of rope. Often nuts just see how far they can throw a welly, so if you want to see who the champion welly-thrower is among your friends, find one or two Wellington boots and a few markers, and go to a place where there's some room. BUT do watch out for old ladies, and anyone else who might not appreciate being hit by a lot of nuts in May – or June, or whenever you decide to do it.

SILLY HIDE-AND-SEEK

To make your friends think you've gone completely mad, get them to play this cranky game. You should have some odd objects which can be tied or pinned to you – things like a dandelion, or a vest or a tea strainer. Hide one somewhere in the house. The person who finds it has to shout 'SILLY' and pin the object onto his or her body. While everyone else counts to twenty, this person then hides the next odd object and waits while the others search for it. Those with objects on them should do their waiting out in the front garden where everyone can see them!

ON THE SHELF

Those books on your shelf – are you fed up with looking at them, and wondering why they don't seem funnier, or more useful? Perhaps it's just that you never find one you want to read? Well, you can brighten things up if you write your own books instead of reading other people's. Just get all those jokes you have collected and try to put them into sections: that is, see if they're 'Animal Jokes' or 'Ghost Jokes', etc. When you've got enough of each sort you can put them into a bigger book and arrange them in alphabetical order. For example – Animals, Cannibals, Cars, Doctors, Ghosts, Monsters, Teachers, Waiters. If all this seems too much trouble, just put them all in a big book, and give it a funny title. Your title can suit the sort of jokes in the book or just be silly, like all the others below. If you get enough titles you can even have a book of *them* and give it a title:

HOW TO BE FUNNY by *Jess Joe King*

NAPOLEON'S ONLY DEFEAT by *Peter Retreat*

HOW TO KEEP THE RAIN OUT by *Anna Rack*

PLAN A VEGETABLE GARDEN by *Rosa Carrots*

HOW TO APOLOGISE by *Thayer Thorry*

A FALL FROM THE CLIFF by *Eileen Dover*

WHAT'S UP, DOC? by *Howie Dewin*

ARITHMETIC SIMPLIFIED by *Lois Carmen Denominator*

WHO KILLED CAIN? by *Howard I. Know*

PUBLIC ENEMY by *Watts E. Dunn*

EARLY RISER by *R. U. Upjohn*

THE MYSTERY OF THE FRUIT MACHINE by *Jack Potts*

ROUND THE MOUNTAIN by *Sheila B. Cumming*

THE STAFF OF LIFE by *Roland Butter*

HOW TO BECOME AN OXFORD BLUE by *Rowan Daly*

THE MAN WHO COULD WORK MIRACLES by *Betty Cant*

YOU NEED INSURANCE by *Justin Case*

MY LIFE OF CRIME by *Robin Banks*

MY LIFE OF DEBT by *Elwys Owen*

MY DEPARTED LOVER by *Hamish Hugh*

PREPARE TO REPENT by *Celeste Chance*

PICTURE POWER

Another way of keeping your friends laughing is by drawing clever pictures that tell a joke. They can be like newspaper cartoons, or they can be like the one below, which is an illustration of one of the jokes from the 'Ridiculous Riddles' section.

It doesn't matter if you're no good at drawing – just do match-men. You can also draw 'Daft Definitions' pictures. Use one of your own definitions, or find one from the 'Daft Definitions' section and do a picture-joke, like the ones on the next page:

PIGSTY

DANDELION

NIGHTMARE

HOW TO DRAW CARTOONS OF PEOPLE YOU KNOW

Drawing cartoons of people is more difficult, but it's worth trying, because it always amuses everyone. It's always easier to draw cartoons of older people's faces, because they're usually more fixed and original than younger faces. But you can draw cartoons of your friends if you draw full-figure ones, rather than just heads.

First, try to decide what's the really unique thing about the person you're drawing. If it's your brother, maybe he has very long legs, or very curly hair, or always wears a football jersey. Or maybe he has a habit, such as biting his nails, or saying 'Er ...' So – draw a pin man, with curly hair or long legs (be sure to make the hair really curly and the legs ridiculously long) – and you'll have a cartoon likeness of him.

If you want to draw a cartoon of a face, watch your subject very closely. Look at your auntie and try and decide what her most characteristic features are – what makes her different from other people. Maybe she has a big nose, or a wide smile, or a gap between her teeth. Whatever it is, exaggerate it so it's really striking.

But here's a word of warning – people usually accept full-figure cartoons of themselves easily enough – especially if you don't bother much about drawing the details of the faces. But when you try to do cartoons of faces alone, they might be a little bit more sensitive!

Auntie Flo

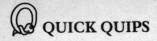

You learnt those Long Jokes for when you had plenty of time to entertain your friends, but there are moments when Quick Quips are the only thing – you can always fit in a few between lessons at school, for instance!

These jokes also come in handy immediately after a long story, or a trick or a game that hasn't worked properly. Or, if you go to the dentist and he's feeling a bit down in the mouth, tell him a few quickies to cheer him up:

See your tailor – and have a fit!

A myth is a lady with a lisp but no husband.

I get on a ferry and every time it makes me cross.

A skeleton is a someone with his outside off.

I'm not saying my cellar's damp, but when I put down a mousetrap I caught a fish!

When I was at school I was teacher's pet. She couldn't afford a dog.

'The refuse-men are here.'
'Tell them we don't need any.'

Advice to worms – sleep late!

'Waiter, bring me some turtle soup – and make it snappy!'

'I don't like cabbage, and I'm glad I don't like it because if I did, I'd eat it – and I hate the stuff!'

A bird in the hand makes it hard to blow your nose.

'I don't care who you are, Fatso – get those reindeer off my roof!'

I say, I say – have you heard about the umbrella salesman who saved his money for a sunny day?

If you show me a thirsty tailor, I'll show you a dry cleaner.

A scrambler's a motorbike that can cook eggs.

If a diver works extra hours, he gets paid undertime.

If a plug doesn't fit – socket!

Baby budgerigars are called budgets.

RIDICULOUS RIDDLES

What is a riddle? The dictionary defines it as a 'conundrum', which is a great help as long as you know what a conundrum is. If you look up 'conundrum', it says 'riddle'!

A riddle is a question with a clever or a witty answer. The question might be:

'Where do all good turkeys go when they die?'
The witty thinker should reply:
'To oven, of course!'

'Oven' is near enough to 'heaven' to be quite a good pun. If you don't know what a pun is, turn back to 'Best Bad Jokes' and you'll find an explanation. Like the Bad Joke, the riddle often uses a pun. When you come to make up riddles, think of some clever puns. If you're very good, you might be able to find a pun with three meanings:

'What do you call a statue of a soldier with its gun and arms missing?'
And the answer is, ' 'armless!'

He's without his arms, without his gun – also called an 'arm' – and he's harmless without any weapon. You can be just as clever with simpler puns. Have a look at the ones in the riddles on the next few pages and you'll soon get the idea.

What squeals more loudly than a pig with a toothache?
Two pigs with toothache.

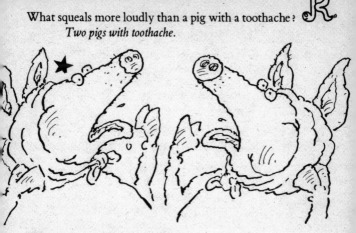

When is water like a Scotsman?
When it's piping hot.

What made the Tower of Pisa lean?
It stopped eating spaghetti.

Why is it a waste of time sending a telegram to
Washington?
Because he's dead.

Do hands grow on trees?
Yes – palm trees.

What bird will never get the vote?
A Mynah, because he'll always be too young.

Why is a vampire a cheap date?
Because he eats necks to nothing.

What's black and white and red all over?
An embarrassed zebra.

What did the Mona Lisa say to the gallery attendant?
I've been framed.

What dance do tin-openers do?
The Can-Can.

Why didn't the little pigs listen to their dad?
Because he was a boar.

What's got teeth but can't bite?
A comb.

What did the cannibal have for supper?
Baked beings on toast.

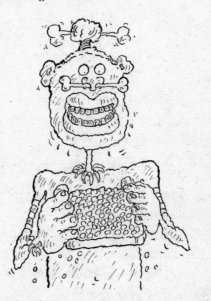

What hangs in a fruit tree and shouts for help?
A damson in distress.

What's the best thing to do with a blue apple?
Cheer it up.

What is the cheapest way to get to China?
Be born there.

What can you put in a glass but not take out of it?
>A crack.

★

What is a volcano?
>A mountain with hiccups.

★

What grows up and grows down at the same time?
>A baby duckling.

★

What did the old man do when he thought he was dying?
>>Went and sat in the living room.

★

What did one strawberry say to the other strawberry?
>'If it wasn't for you we wouldn't be in this jam.'

★

Is it best to write on an empty or a full stomach?
>Neither – it's best to use paper.

★

Why was the insect kicked out of the forest?
>Because it was a litterbug.

★

What is a fast duck?
>A quick quack.

Why did the old man put wheels on his rocking chair?
>Because he wanted to rock and roll.

★

What do you call a magician with a helicopter?
>A flying saucerer.

★

Why are sheep always short of money?
>Because they're always being fleeced.

★

Why couldn't the dog catch his tail?
>Because it is hard to make ends meet these days.

★

What has four fingers and a thumb but is not a hand?
>A glove.

SIGNS OF THE TIMES

Watch out for funny signs! They're everywhere, and looking out for them can shorten a long car journey. Persuade your parents to give a prize for the funniest sign, and, if you can manage to, write down all the good ones so that you can add them to your books of jokes when you get back home. The signs may be funny on their own, or they may be funny because of their position. For example someone passed a pub recently which was called The Omnibus Inn. It had a sign outside which said 'NO COACHES'!

Here are some other examples:

DUE TO A STRIKE, GRAVEDIGGING WILL BE DONE BY A SKELETON CREW

Horse Manure
A filled bag, 25p
Do it yourself, 15p

DANCE DISCOTHEQUE
Highly Exclusive
ALL WELCOME

BRING YOUR LUGGAGE TO US –
WE WILL SEND IT IN ALL DIRECTIONS

LADIES MAY HAVE FITS UPSTAIRS

HOLES PAINTED WHITE NOT TO BE DUG

CUSTOMERS WHO FIND OUR STAFF RUDE SHOULD WAIT AND SEE THE MANAGER

PLEASE IN CASE OF FIRE DO YOUR BEST TO ALARM THE HALL PORTER

TRADITIONS

On a rainy day, why not invent some traditions? This may sound impossible, but if you think of some real traditions like the Changing of the Guard, or the tradition of ducking people in the village pond at certain times of the year, or beating the parish boundary, you will probably be able to come up with your own. There's no need for the ceremony to mean anything, though it's fun inventing reasons for each odd action.

Here are a couple to give you the idea. You are advised NOT to try them out!

HATNIP-CHUCKING

This age-old tradition has been handed down from father to son, and handed back up again when the son found out what a hatnip was. It's a cross between a bowler hat and a turnip. The traditional way of making one is to get a bowler hat and cut it into little pieces. In the old days these pieces were mixed with brown sauce and radishes. This was because when food was scarce people ate their bowler hats rather than go hungry, but they had to mix the pieces with brown sauce and radishes as bowler hats really don't taste very good on their own.

After the hat is cut up, the turnip is cut in half and its centre scooped out. The bowler hat mixture is put into the scooped-out bits. Then the two halves of the turnip are put back together, and stuck up with sticky tape.

The hatnip is now complete and ready to be chucked.

The tradition originated in London. Once upon a time the streets of London were so dirty and so full of rubbish that people threw things to each other across the street instead of stepping through all the mess. When someone was very hungry and had run out of bowler hats and turnips, he or she would ring a bell and open the window, hopefully. Any of the neighbours across the street who had some spare, and who wanted a bit of fun, would try to chuck a hatnip through the open window across the street.

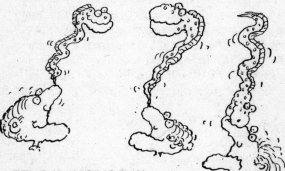

EEL-BALANCING DAY

The 30th of February is Eel-Balancing Day. This ancient custom takes place at a very secret place where certain people whose names begin with 'O' have to balance eels on the tips of their noses. However, before they can do this they have to catch their eels. Let us listen to the words of Oliver Oldham – he's now 96, but remembers going out to catch his eels as a young man:

'Oh, ar, we used ter go out before dawn, and we used ter creep through the shallow water looking out for them snoozing eels. When I saw one, I'd get me net right under 'im, tickle his tummy for a bit, then, just as 'e was 'avin' a nice dream, whip 'im out o' the water and into a big tank …'

This tank would then be carried back to the secret place, as long as someone could remember where it was, and the carriers sang the traditional Eel-Balancer's Song on the way:

'You have to bring the eel to heel
    And get his toes upon your nose
And balance him up with loads of zeal
    And get to the Cow afore it close.'

The 'Cow' mentioned in the last line is not an animal but a place of refreshment, and the meaning is that the balancing has to be completed and the eels put back into the water in time for everyone to get to the Dun Cow pub for a little something. Anyone who fails to reach the 'Cow' in time has to run through a goldfish pond six times wearing a kilt and a large brown paper bag.

Eel-balancing is still carried on, according to Oliver Oldham, but the place where it is supposed to take place is now so secret that hardly anyone ever finds it.

OPEN A FOLK MUSEUM

Traditions are connected with folk-lore, and things of the countryside generally. A lot of work has been done all over the country to collect folk stories and traditions, as well as all the bits and pieces, like old ploughs and kitchen ware, that go with them. It's become big business and thousands of people visit Folk Museums every year.

But some of the bits and pieces are so small or so odd that they really could be anything. So, why not open your own Folk Museum? You'll soon find funny things to exhibit, as the idea is to give everything a really complicated label. You can put anything on show – as long as the label is convincing, who'll be able to tell the difference between your stuff and the real thing?

Early False teeth
Possibly Stone Age

note Leonardo teeth marks

Leonardo Da vinci Pencil.

— smartie belonging to <u>Shirley Temple</u>.

— *note* sucked white.

A carrot that was nibbled by <u>Bugs Bunny</u>.

Charge 5p admission and offer special souvenirs (like 'A Piece of Old England' for £5 – which is just a matchbox full of earth).

UNWELL, WELL, WELL …

Cheer yourself up if you're ill! Cheer up a friend if he's ill! Cheer up the doctor if he's ill! Only, take care not to overdo it – he might die laughing …

★

PATIENT: 'Will my chickenpox be better by next week?'
DOCTOR: 'I'm afraid I can't make rash promises.'

★

'Doctor, doctor, I keep seeing red and yellow flags.'
'Have you seen a psychiatrist?'
'No. Just red and yellow flags.'

★

OPTICIAN: 'You think you have bad eyesight? Well, just read the line of letters on the bottom of that card.'
PATIENT: 'What card?'

'Doctor, my family think I'm mad because I like bananas.'
'Oh, that's perfectly normal – I like bananas, too.'
'Do you? You must come round and see my collection – I've got thousands!'

'Madam, your husband must have absolute rest.'
'But doctor, he won't listen to me ...'
'Well, that's a good start.'

✦

'Did you take your husband's temperature as I told you, Mrs Murphy?'
'Yes indeed, doctor, I put a barometer on his chest, and it said "very dry" so I bought him a pint of beer, and he's gone back to work.'

'Oh doctor, I'm so sorry to drag you all this way into the country on such a bad night.'
'That's all right – I have another patient near here, so I can kill two birds with one stone.'

✦

The pretty girl had been examined by the doctor.
'You've got acute appendicitis,' he said at last.
'Doctor, I've come here to be examined, not admired,' said the young lady.

✦

YOUNG DOCTOR: 'Why do you always ask patients what they had for their dinner?'
OLD DOCTOR: 'Well, according to their menus, I make out my bills.'

'Well, madam, what is the matter with your husband?'
'I'm afraid, doctor, he's worrying about money.'
'Ah! I think I can relieve him of that.'

'You need glasses,' said the doctor.
'But I'm wearing glasses,' said the patient.
'In that case,' said the doctor, 'I need glasses.'

FARMER PATIENT: 'And how's lawyer Smith,
doctor?'
DOCTOR: 'He's lying at death's door, I'm afraid.'
FARMER: 'Yes – at death's door – and still lying.'

**The medical paper asked: 'What would you do
in the case of a person eating poisonous
mushrooms?'**
**The student wrote: 'Recommend a change of
diet.'**

DOCTOR: 'Well, Willie, how are you today?'
WILLIE: 'All right, I guess, doctor, but I'm having
trouble with my breathing.'
DOCTOR: 'I must see if I can give you something to
stop that.'

SOME INTERESTING ILLNESSES

strained clavichord
sponge fingers (a Victorian ailment)
fish fingers
weasels (like measles only with spots *and* fur)
Kentucky-fried chickenpox
pink fever (a mild form of scarlet fever)
drastic gastric flu (patient is laid low)
elastic gastric flu (patient is laid wall-to-wall)
plastic gastric flu (patient is not bio-degradable)

HEDGEHOG (to his friend Freddy Frog): 'At least you're in there with a chance; whoever heard of a princess kissing a hedgehog?'

A pretty girl went into a dress shop, and asked the assistant if she could try on the dress in the window. 'I wish you would,' said the assistant, 'it would be very good for business.'

WATER BAILIFF: 'You can't fish without a permit.'
ANGLER: 'Oh, it's all right thanks, I'm doing fine with this worm.'

Paddy was marooned on a desert island. One day the tide brought in a canoe, so Paddy broke it up and made himself a raft.

BOOK SALESMAN: 'This book will do half your work for you.'
BUSINESSMAN: 'Good. I'll take two.'

'What would I get,' enquired the man who had just insured his property against fire, 'if this building should burn down tonight?'

'I would say,' replied the insurance agent, 'about ten years.'

★

TEACHER: 'Ben, why don't you wash your face? I can see what you had for breakfast this morning.'
BEN: 'What was it, Teacher?'
TEACHER: 'Egg.'
BEN: 'Wrong, Teacher. That was yesterday.'

ROBERTA: 'Will you take me for a drive on Sunday?'
ROBERT: 'Yes, but suppose it rains?'
ROBERTA: 'Well, in that case, come the day before.'

★

MARY: 'Do you allow a man to kiss you when you're out motoring with him?'
JANE: 'Certainly not. If a man can drive safely while kissing me, he's not giving the kiss the attention it deserves.'

VERSE AND WORSE

Potty poems, loony limericks and odd odes of every kind are very useful to know when you want to be funny. You can whisper these verses in the quiet bits of horror films, or sing them in the swimming pool, or write them in people's autograph books. They're bound to cause a titter or two whatever you do with them!

★

There was a young lady named Rose,
Who had a huge wart on her nose.
   When she had it removed
   Her appearance improved,
But her glasses slipped down to her toes.

★

There was a strange fellow from Cork,
Who took his pet toad for a walk.
   When they asked, 'Is it tame?'
   He replied, 'Yes, its name
Is Therese and it lives upon pork.'

There was a young man from Nepal,
Who was asked to a fancy-dress ball.
   He said, 'Oh, I'll risk it
   And go as a biscuit.'
But the dog ate him up in the hall.

★

There was a young lady of Leeds,
Who swallowed a packet of seeds.
   In a month, silly lass,
   She was covered with grass,
And she couldn't sit down for the weeds.

There was a young man called Davy,
Who hated the food in the Navy.
　　He couldn't have beef,
　　In case his false teeth
Would drop out and fall in the gravy.

There was a young man of Devizes,
Whose ears were of different sizes.
　　The one that was small
　　Was no use at all,
But the other won several prizes.

I wish I had your picture,
　　It would be very nice.
I'd hang it in the attic
　　To scare away the mice.

If you build a better mousetrap,
　　And put it in your house,
Before long, Mother Nature
　　Will build a better mouse.

A major, with wonderful force,
Called out in Hyde Park for a horse.
　　All the flowers looked round,
　　But no horse could be found,
So he just rhododendron, of course.

History's a dreadful subject,
Dead as it can be.
Once it killed the Romans,
And now it's killing me.

Willie poisoned his father's tea;
    Father died in agony.
Mother came, and looked quite vexed:
    'Really, Will,' she said, 'what next?'

Into the cistern little Willie
Pushed his little sister Lily.
Mother couldn't find our daughter:
Now we sterilise our water.

A flea and a fly met in a flue,
Said the flea to the fly, 'What shall we do?'
    'Let's flee,' said the fly.
    'Let's fly,' said the flea.
And they flew through a flaw in the flue.

Here lies the body of Anna,
Done to death by a banana.
It wasn't the fruit that laid her low,
But the skin of the thing that made her go.

I eat my peas with honey,
I've done it all my life.
It makes the peas taste funny,
But it keeps them on the knife!

The Awful Adventures of Fergus on his School Trip to London

Little Fergus was a brat
The whole of London wondered at.
He dropped a stink-bomb in St Paul's
Just to see how fast it falls.
He caught a raven in the Tower,
And covered it with glue and flour –
Until Beefeaters nabbed him quick
And said, 'A raven lunatic!'
Next, Fergus in Trafalgar Square
Pea-shootered all the pigeons there,
And up old Nelson's column shinned
To wave a conker in the wind.
When Fergus sang outside the Ritz,
The windows splintered into bits.
And when he whistled in the Zoo
The beasts all started howling, too.
Next Fergus sauntered to Tussaud's
To see the waxen Queens and Lords,
But in the Horror-Chamber grim
The public all recoiled at *him*.
'It's time for home,' his teacher said.
'We've painted this old town quite red!
So come on children, mount the bus!'
Said Fergus, 'They'll remember US!!'

WORD FUN

Some words – like 'pong' or 'ichthyosaurus' – just
sound funny without your having to do anything with
them. However, you won't be thought very funny if
you stand and say, 'zeuglodontoid' or 'inconcinnity' –
that is, if you can say them! You'll probably just get a
bucket of ice-cold water thrown over you, so why not
try the games here? Word Riddles are like ordinary
riddles. Instead of a pun, they are letter jokes. If you
have a look at them, you'll soon understand how they
work. With the Word Quiz, you have to choose the
right meaning for the given word. This gets quite
difficult, but don't worry if you can't do them – the
wrong meanings are quite amusing, and you can make
up your own word quizzes with funny definitions as
soon as you've looked at a few of the ones here.

WORD RIDDLES

How can you spell 'chilly' with two letters?
> *I. C.*

What letter stands for a drink?
> *The letter T.*

What did the boy say when he opened his piggy bank
and found nothing?
> *O.I.C.U.R.M.T.*

How can you spell 'rot' with two letters?
> *D. K.*

What letter is like a vegetable?
> *The letter P.*

What word grows smaller when you add two letters to it?

> *Add 'er' to short and it becomes shorter.*

How many letters are there in the alphabet?

> *Eleven. T-H-E A-L-P-H-A-B-E-T.*

Why is the letter B hot?

> *Because it makes oil boil.*

What is never out of sight?

> *The letter S.*

What is the beginning of eternity,
  The end of time and space;
The beginning of every end,
  And the end of every race?

> *The letter E.*

When is it correct to say, 'I is?'

> *'I is the letter after H.'*

Why is the letter N the most powerful letter?

> *Because it's in the middle of TNT.*

What roman numeral can climb a wall?

> *IV.*

How do you spell 'we' with two letters without using the letters W and E?

> *U and I.*

How do you spell 'very happy' with three letters?

> *X. T. C.*

If you add 2-forget and 2-forget, what do you get?

> *4-gotten.*

WORD QUIZ

Test your word-power and make yourself laugh with this crazy word quiz. The words get more difficult as you go along.

1. What is a BUNION?
    (a)   a sort of Italian onion
    (b)   an Easter cake
    (c)   a painful lump on your foot
    (d)   a baby's toy

2. What is to THROTTLE?
    (a)   to dance energetically
    (b)   to strangle somebody
    (c)   to rinse a bottle
    (d)   to fish for squid

3. What is a FENDER?
    (a)   the surround to a fireplace
    (b)   someone who saves penalties
    (c)   a sort of cucumber
    (d)   a defence lawyer

4. What is SHINGLE?
   (a) a food like porridge
   (b) a rock group
   (c) a game played in Ireland
   (d) pebbles on the beach

5. What is a PREDICTION?
   (a) something long and slimy in the undergrowth
   (b) a strong drink
   (c) a special way of speaking
   (d) a forecast for the future

6. What is GORGONZOLA?
   (a) a mad monster living in a Greek cave
   (b) a sort of Italian cheese
   (c) a French novelist living on the dole
   (d) the name of one of the Queen's corgis

7. What is a MANDOLIN?
   (a) a strange stringed instrument
   (b) a little orange from Seville
   (c) a strange little monkey
   (d) a sticking plaster

8. What is a CORNUCOPIA?
   (a) a photocopying machine
   (b) a cure for hard skin on the feet
   (c) a horn of plenty
   (d) a man with a horse's legs

9. What is HYPOCHONDRIA?
   (a) fear of dogs
   (b) a Roman central-heating system
   (c) fear of central heating
   (d) thinking you're ill when you're not

10. What is a SQUINT?
    (a) a baby octopus
    (b) a firework
    (c) an irregularity of the eyes
    (d) an Ethiopian coin

11. What is CROQUET?
    (a) a kind of knitting
    (b) a potato rissole
    (c) a tall hat
    (d) a ball and hoop game

12. What is a QUADRUPED?
    (a) a college playground
    (b) something folded four times
    (c) an animal with four legs
    (d) a mountain pass

13. What is a GROTTO?
- (a) the part of a town occupied by racial minorities
- (b) an underground cavern
- (c) an Italian dish
- (d) a musical instrument

14. What is a QUAIL?
- (a) a feathered pen
- (b) a shiver down your spine
- (c) a bird
- (d) a quantity of paper

15. What is a VIPER?
- (a) a cleaning cloth
- (b) a poisonous snake
- (c) a stage whisper
- (d) part of a lady's underclothes

16. What is a VALISE?
- (a) a gentleman's servant
- (b) a regiment of the Guards
- (c) a mattress made of straw
- (d) a suitcase

17. What is PLATINUM?
- (a) a fountain pen
- (b) the largest possible number of something
- (c) a metal
- (d) a web-footed animal

18. What is a TUMBRIL?
- (a) a machine used for drying laundry
- (b) a wagon used in the French Revolution
- (c) the icy wastes of the Frozen North
- (d) an acrobat

19. What is an ANAGRAM?
    (a)   a great-grandmother
    (b)   an old-fashioned record-player
    (c)   a district between France and Spain
    (d)   letters in a word rearranged to make
           another word

20. What is a RESOLUTION?
    (a)   an uprising
    (b)   a recollection
    (c)   determination
    (d)   the agenda of a meeting

21. What is a GOURMAND?
    (a)   a greedy eater
    (b)   a plant similar to a cucumber
    (c)   a pigsty
    (d)   a type of goldfish

22. What is an EGRESS?
    (a) a baby eagle
    (b) a species of heron
    (c) a black lady
    (d) an outlet or exit

23. What is a BUSTARD?
    (a) a yellow sauce
    (b) a hot condiment
    (c) a bird similar to an ostrich
    (d) a jerkin made of buckskin

24. What is ORATORY?
    (a) a church collection
    (b) a figurative manner of speaking or writing
    (c) an eloquent speech
    (d) a sandy patch of earth

25. What is a COCOON?
    (a) a subdivision of a regiment
    (b) a ribbon stuck in a hat like a badge
    (c) a covering spun by certain insects for protection
    (d) a bird which nests in the nests of other birds

ANSWERS TO WORD QUIZ

1. (c)
2. (b)
3. (a)
4. (d)
5. (d)
6. (b)
7. (a)
8. (c)
9. (d)
10. (c)
11. (d)
12. (c)
13. (b)
14. (c)
15. (b)
16. (d)
17. (c)
18. (b)
19. (d)
20. (c)
21. (a)
22. (d)
23. (c)
24. (c)
25. (c)

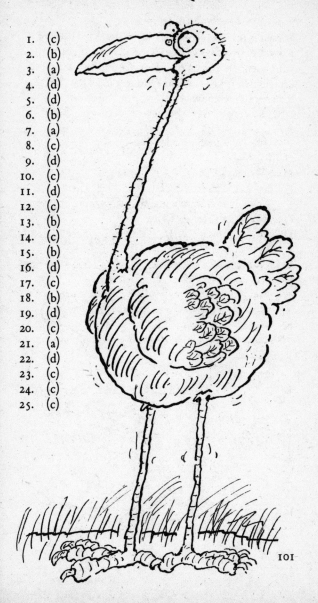

X = DASH · DOT · DOT · DASH ·

Some jokes are so good you only want to tell them to a few select friends — so write them in code. If you give your friends a copy of the Morse Code below they can decipher your joke and have fun sending back one of theirs — if they know any!

A	· —
B	— · · ·
C	— · — ·
D	— · ·
E	·
F	· · — ·
G	— — ·
H	· · · ·
I	· ·
J	· — — —
K	— · —
L	· — · ·
M	— —
N	— ·
O	— — —
P	· — — ·
Q	— — · —
R	· — ·
S	· · ·
T	—
U	· · —
V	· · · —
W	· — —
X	— · · —
Y	— · — —
Z	— — · ·

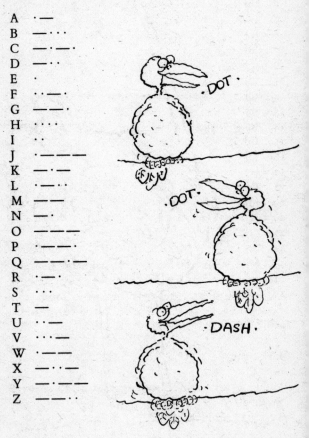

. DOT .

. DOT .

. DASH .

102

Figures: 1 ·————   6 —····
2 ··—
 —— 7 ——···
3 ···—
 — 8 ———··
4 ····—9 ————·
5 ····· 0 —————

See if you can decipher this quip:

—·—·/·—·/—·/—·/—··/·—·/·//·/···//
——/·—/—·—·/·//·—··/···/——·/
····/—·//——·/·/·—·/—··/···//

Remember that one stroke means a new letter, and two strokes mean a new word.

You can invent your own codes. You could try using numbers for letters, for example:

A = 5	F = 12	K = 4
B = 8	G = 2	L = 19
C = 24	H = 7	M = 21
D = 18	I = 3	N = 26
E = 13	J = 10	

and so on. You needn't just use the numbers 1–26; any range can be used. Make sure you have a name for each of the codes so that when you send a joke to someone you can indicate which code it's in. Then your friend will get the joke, and not a piece of nonsense.

Incidentally …

FRED: 'What sort of illness does a Secret Agent have all the time?'
TED: 'A code in the nose!'

YULE LAUGH AT THIS

Christmas is a great time for traditional fun. After Christmas dinner everyone probably falls asleep, having eaten too much of everything; but when the family has had a doze, get Christmas Day going again with an imaginative game of

CHARADES

You have to choose an action – such as pulling in a ship's anchor, or being a taxi-driver and picking up a passenger – and act it out as well as you can. When you've done your bit, and everyone's crying, 'Brilliant!' or 'Get off!', you must demand to know from them what it was you were doing. Whoever guesses has to act out the next charade.

If everyone's just too tired to move, you can describe what you would have done had you not had that fourth helping of pudding. These charades can be much more complicated, and to get you going, here are some examples:

CHARADE NO. 1

'I'm crouched on the table and curled up into a ball. There's steam rising from my body, and custard running down my neck from the large dollop on my head. What am I?'
WHAT THEY'LL SAY:
    'You're a Christmas Pudding!'
YOUR ANSWER:
    'No. I'm Mount Etna after an eruption!'

CHARADE NO. 2

Stretch out flat on the table. Get your little sister to pull your feet and your big brother to pull your hands. Then you go BANG! and they both fall backwards.
WHAT THEY'LL SAY:
  'You're a cracker!'
YOUR ANSWER:
  'It's very nice of you to say so, but we were enacting the splitting of the atom.'

CAROL CHARADES

Another sort of charade is where you act out the title of a carol, e.g. 'The Boar's Head'.

When Uncle Pete is droning on: 'We thought we'd take the A6097 to Much Crashing but we missed the turn and found ourselves on the Great Snoring bypass and so we had to take the B7432 to Milton Windwiper and that put an extra 20 minutes on ...'

Place Uncle Pete's head on a serving-dish (you can detach it from his body if you really want to cheer the family up!). And there you have it: 'The Bore's Head'!

Or you can try 'Ding Dong Merrily on High'.

Send your sister and her boyfriend up onto the landing and as they leave the room, whisper to your sister, 'I saw him with Rita Tweeter the other night.' Soon, they'll be having a fine old row up there.

'You told me you had an Evening Class on Thursdays.'

'Well, I do.'

'What's all this about Rita, then? You pig!'

'There's no need to fly off the handle. You're so jealous!'

And here, to the listening family downstairs, it's clear: there's a 'Ding Dong Merrily on High'.

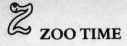

ZOO TIME

Zoos are full of animals who know how to be funny without really trying. Penguins waddle, monkeys leap about and the sea-lions make funny honking noises.

Here are some games for zoo time, or any time you want to be as funny as the funniest animals in the zoo.

IMITATIONS

Straight imitations of animals make a good party game, and if you develop your own skills you can amuse your friends any time with your impressions of the zoo!

MIME

Try showing how an animal would do an everyday thing. You don't make a single noise. Get your friends to guess what the animal is, and when they do, get them to do a mime. Here are a few suggestions to get things going:

A pig cooking an omelette.
A frog sweeping the floor.

A horse going shopping in a supermarket.
A chicken at a disco.

A monkey playing tennis.
A snake watching TV.
A crocodile working in the garden.

A cat posting a letter.
A dog playing the cello.
A goldfish doing a crossword puzzle.

A budgie cleaning windows.

IMITATING ANIMALS WITH NOISES ONLY

This is easier than mime, and it can cause more hilarious havoc – so don't go mad and start imitating elephants trumpeting if you're in the library! If you've got a tape-recorder, record some of your animal imitations and see if your friends can recognise them. If you haven't got one, stand behind the door so they can't see you. (They'll probably find this much more enjoyable!)

Once you've mastered the art of animal imitations, you can act out short charades based on stories, plays or songs in which animals have leading roles. Your friends have got to try to guess the title from your two-minute version. (Use animal noises and mime only, to make it more difficult!)

Some simple ones:

Dick Whittington
The Muppets
Mother Goose
The Teddy-Bears' Picnic
The Wind in the Willows
Alice in Wonderland
Noah's Flood

Then, try acting two-minute charades of well-known proverbs or sayings involving animals. Some examples:

A bird in the hand is worth two in the bush.
Let sleeping dogs lie.
You can take a horse to water but you can't make it drink.
Don't look a gift horse in the mouth.
When the cat's away the mice will play.
A bear with a sore head.
A cat may look at a queen.

OLD JOKES ABOUT ANIMALS

There are lots of good old jokes about animals, and some pretty funny new ones, too. Learn a few of them off by heart and try them out next time you go to the zoo. Or don't wait that long, try them out on your family. They're animals, too, you know!

What's black and white with red spots?
A zebra with measles.

On which side does a chicken have the most feathers?
On the outside.

When is a black dog not a black dog?
When he's a greyhound.

What is a parrot?
A wordy birdie.

What is a calf after it is six months old?
Seven months old.

What did the mother worm say to her baby when he was late for breakfast?
'Where in earth have you been?'

What keys are furry?
Donkeys.

Did you hear about the man who thought that the Rover 3500 was a bionic dog?

Learn these rhymes and cheer everyone's flagging spirits as they look at yet another kind of ant in the Insect House!

Ooey Gooey was a worm,
   And a fine young worm was he.
He ventured on the railway track
   The train he did not see.
EEk! Ouch! Splatter, splutter!
Ooey Gooey's peanut butter.

I raised such a hullaballoo,
When I found a big mouse in my stew;
   Said the waiter, 'Don't shout
   And wave it about,
Or the rest will be wanting one, too!'

A wonderful bird is the sea gull.
It can fly quite as high as an eagle.
   It will sit on the sand,
   And eat from your hand,
But you can't tell a he from a she gull.

A furry old bear at the Zoo
Could always find something to do.
   When it bored him to go
   On a walk to and fro,
He went backwards and walked fro and to.

A centipede named Marguerite
Bought shoes for each one of her feet.
   'For,' she said, 'I might chance
   To go to a dance,
And I must have my outfit complete.'

A mouse in the night woke Miss Dowd,
She was frightened and screamed very loud.
   Then she thought: 'At the least
   I shall scare off the beast.'
And she sat up in bed and meowed.

Hickory, dickory, dock:
The mice ran up the clock!
The clock struck one –
The rest escaped with minor injuries.

PS.

You may have reached the end of this book feeling no
funnier than you did at the beginning. There is no cause
for alarm. Being funny takes practice, years and years
of practice, so if you haven't yet mastered the art of
turning your audience into a quivering mass of helpless
laughter the moment you start telling them a joke, don't
despair. Keep reading *How to be Funny* and in time
they'll find you *hysterical*.

Don't worry if at first it's hard,
And the laughs you get are few –
Remember that the mighty oak
Was once a nut like you!

A book like this should end on a high note, so here it is: